# *From* STEAMBOATS *to* SUBCHASERS

## A History of the Shelburne Shipyard

### JERRY ASKE, JR.

ONION RIVER PRESS

Burlington, Vermont

# From STEAMBOATS to SUBCHASERS

A
History
of the
Shelburne
Shipyard

JERRY ASKE, JR.

From Steamboats to Subchasers, *A History of the Shelburne Shipyard*

Copyright © 2012 by L. Jerome Aske, Jr.

Cover illustration copyright © 2012 by Billy Brauer.

Book design by Laurie Thomas

Published by Onion River Press
214 Maple Street, Suite 214
Burlington, Vermont, 05401
www.onionriverpress.com

ISBN: 978-1-957184-30-2

Library of Congress Control Number: 2023909303

Originally Published by Red Barn Books of Vermont,
an imprint of Wind Ridge Publishing, Inc.
ISBN: 978-1-935922-14-8

*To my father, Lambert Jerome "Jerry" Aske, Sr.,
whose vision and talents gave new life to the already
historic Shelburne Shipyard.*

Askes—seniors and junior. From left: Dad, me, and Uncle Wendell.

# Acknowledgements

Thanks to the late Gardiner Lane, whose request for help with his research paper on the Shipyard was the catalyst for me to write my own book. Thanks to the late Ralph Nading Hill, who opened his own card files for me to use when writing a paper on the Shipyard for a college course, and was a lifelong stimulant and role model for my own interest in the lake. The late Al Greenberg, former editor-in-chief of *Skiing Magazine,* can be credited with boosting my confidence as a writer by publishing several of my articles.  Many thanks, too, to the countless number of friends and acquaintances who, responding to one of my many tales on the subject, said, "You oughta write a book!"

# Introduction

Let's steam down Lake Champlain together, by sidewheeler and naval warship, enjoying what the Native American god Odzihozo thought were the world's most spectacular views—the majestic Adirondacks to the west and the glorious Green Mountains to the east.

That mighty Abenaki god was so impressed with our lovely lake and her environs that he chose to submerge himself in her depths, his head and shoulders above water, so that he could remain here, soaking up the beauty for all eternity. We know Odzihozo now as the tiny island called Rock Dunder, which is visible from the Burlington ferry docks.

Writing about the Aske years at the Shelburne Shipyard has been an exhilarating experience, but it never could have happened if my friend Gardiner Lane had not come to me for help some years ago. Gardiner was writing a paper on the Shelburne Shipyard for a course at the Maritime Museum. The paper was moving right along, as he told the shipyard history in chronological fashion, until he came to the 1940s. He found nothing anywhere in his research about this period, so Gardiner came to me to help him finish the paper by completing the story.

I found letters and photos and documents about that period, but, more importantly, I reached back in time and found my memory bank was filled to overflowing. I remembered stories, phone conversations, happenings, and my incredible trip down the lake as a nine-year-old on board a naval vessel headed for war. So after I helped Gardiner complete his story, I decided to write my own.

Here it is, for you, for my children, for my grandchildren, and for anyone interested in some pretty good years. Steam ahead!

The Shelburne Shipyard has had its home in the sheltered harbor in Shelburne Bay since the early 1820s, but its story begins even earlier. From 1794 to 1797, the hundred-acre tract of land on the end of Pottier's Point that would become the shipyard's home changed ownership four times. Then, in 1797, Nathan White bought the parcel for $900. When he died in 1826 the land was passed to his eldest son, Andrew, who then sold it to his brothers Robert and Lavater. While most histories that mention the shipyard say that the Lake Champlain Steamboat Company moved its winter quarters from the Otter Creek in Vergennes to the Harbor in 1820, land records show that the Whites owned the land until 1828. In that year they sold a parcel approximately 420 x 130 feet to Cornelius P. Van Ness, a stockholder in the Lake Champlain Steamboat Company. Probably the Steamboat Company leased the land from the Whites prior to that time.

It is known that the steamship *General Greene* was built at the Shelburne site during 1824-1825 for the Champlain Ferry Company, which was newly chartered by the Vermont Legislature to operate boats between Burlington and Port Kent, New York. The deed that records the transfer from the Whites to Van Ness places the parcel about three rods (fifty feet) southerly "of the place where the steamship *General Greene* and the sloop *Bolivar* were built." The master carpenters on the *General Greene* were Messrs. Phillips and White. It is quite possible, indeed probable, that Lavater S. White was the Mr. White mentioned, as he was to be one of the master shipwrights on many of the steamboats built at the yard. Queneska Island, just south of West Beach, was also known as White's Island for many years.

In 1827, a stone shop was built to house the office, power plant, carpentry and machine shops. In addition, a ways was constructed for hauling boats for repairs. Van Ness transferred his ownership of the property to Isaiah Townsend in 1833. Townsend, also one of the original directors of the Lake Champlain Steamboat Company, had purchased the assets of the company in 1831. He then merged his newly acquired property and company with the Champlain Transportation Company.

The shipyard was to remain the property of the Champlain Transportation Company for 113 years until my father, Jerry Aske, Sr., and his brother, Wendell, bought it in 1946. As the Champlain Transportation Company prospered, more land was added to the shipyard in a series of acquisitions. Storehouses, dwellings, and timber sheds were constructed, and the shipyard began to resemble a small village. In the wintertime, when the lake iced over and forced the ships back into the harbor, ship-

*General Greene* was the first steamboat built at Shelburne Shipyard—in 1825.

yard crews would do maintenance work on the hulls and machinery. On good days, when the temperature was not too severe, they would repair and paint the exterior, working from scaffolds erected on the ice. During inclement weather they would perform the necessary maintenance inside, where "donkey boilers" provided heat.

Competition for the increasingly lucrative cargo and passenger trade was stiff and often ruthless. The Champlain Transportation Company became noted for its takeovers, having not only absorbed the Lake Champlain Steamboat Company and the Champlain Ferry Company, but the St. Albans Steamboat Company and several small, private builders as well. In 1836, the company decided to exert its control of the lake and the boat construction business by building the deluxe steamboat *Burlington* at the shipyard. Soon after she began regular service, *Burlington* began to receive glowing reviews, including this one by Charles Dickens after a trip up Lake Champlain on his way from Montreal to New York in 1842:

> The Burlington is a perfectly exquisite achievement of neatness, elegance and order. The decks are drawing rooms; the cabins boudoirs, choicely furnished and adorned with prints, pictures and musical instruments; every nook and corner of this vessel is a perfect curiosity of graceful comfort and beautiful contrivance … By means of this floating palace we were soon in the United States again, and called that evening at Burlington: a pretty town, where we lay an hour or so.

*Jerry Aske, Jr.*

Shipyard crew and boardinghouse staff in front of the boarding house during the early twentieth century. Workmen stayed at the boarding house (now the Shelburne Marina building) during winter months and worked on the steamboats from scaffolds on the ice.

Two years after Dickens' trip, another distinguished visitor, Sir James Lumsden, the Lord Provost of Glasgow, Scotland, recorded the following in his notes:

> We went on board the *Burlington,* one of the most splendid and commodious of steam vessels…The interior decorations are so truly splendid that you might fancy yourself in the drawing room of a ducal palace. The cleanliness of the vessel is the admiration of all strangers. There is no unpleasant shouting or noise. All orders are given by bell signals from the officers on deck; no brawling to the engineer, "stop her, turn ahead, two back strokes," and such vulgar expressions as you hear on board our steamers on the Clyde… Everything on board is clocklike…The men are all trained to their particular duties—every one [sic] at his post—and the discipline equal to that on board a ship-of-war. The arrangements at meals are excellent and the greatest attention paid to the passengers by the stewards, who are numerous and all dressed in neat, clean, fancy uniforms.

Since 1823, a canal to the south had provided navigable waters between New York and Montreal, but with the coming of the railroads in the late 1840s a new

"Business end" of horse-powered skid marine railway. The painstaking process of hauling a steamboat using a skid ways could take up to a week.

*Jerry Aske, Jr.*

competition developed. In 1852, the Rutland and Burlington Railroad bought all the property of the Champlain Transportation Company except for its charter. In 1854, the railroad, finding the venture into the steamboat business a failure, agreed to sell the property back to the Champlain Transportation Company. By 1856, it had regained its monopoly over water transportation.

On December 7, 1870 (exactly seventy-one years to the day before the event that would bring us Askes to the Shelburne Shipyard), the Delaware and Hudson Railroad gained control of the Champlain Transportation Company. This had no effect on the policies of the corporation, nor on the operation or schedules of its boats. However, the directors of the D & H guided the Champlain Transportation Company into a new phase as an excursion line. They curtailed some operations and shortened some runs, substituting an 81-mile cruise between Plattsburgh and Fort Ticonderoga for the former 125-mile trip between Whitehall, New York and St. Jean, Quebec, for example. These changes allowed the company to continue operating despite the fact that by 1875 it was apparent that the heyday of steamboat travel had passed.

*Ticonderoga*, the last sidewheeler to be built on Lake Champlain, was preceded by two similar ships—*Chateaugay* and *Vermont III*—both of which marked a milestone for the shipyard in that their hulls were made of iron. *Chateaugay*'s finest hour came as a result of the 1927 hurricane and flood. Western Vermont was cut off from the outside world; the Rutland and Central Vermont railroads were unable to operate.

Lines connecting the old skid railway to horse-propelled capstans.

Sidewheel steamboats *Chateaugay* and *Vermont III* iced in for the winter, circa 1915.

On the fifth of November, *Chateaugay* steamed out of her winter quarters in Shelburne Harbor on a mission of mercy. For days she carried flood refugees to New York state, returning with food, clothing, mail, and medicine. *Chateaugay* was finally able to return to the shipyard sixteen days later, after the Rutland Railroad restored partial rail service to the region. *Chateaugay's* engines were sold for scrap in 1937, after Horace W. Corbin of South Hero, Vermont, bought the Champlain Transportation Company, and her hull was cut into sections to be transported to Lake Winnipesaukee, New Hampshire, where it was reassembled as a diesel-powered excursion boat. It is still operating there every summer as the motor vessel *Mt. Washington.*

Most of the wooden steamships built at the shipyard during the nineteenth century were stripped of any useable gear and machinery and then cabled to trees at the southern end of the harbor where the remains of their hulls are still visible beneath the water. *Vermont III* was converted to a freighter in 1945 and *Ticonderoga*, the sole surviving Lake Champlain sidewheeler, was transported to the Shelburne Museum in 1954.

No more large vessels were built at the Shelburne Shipyard until 1942 when a Midwestern firm leased the yard and joined the war effort against the Axis powers. A fire in 1910 destroyed the old stone shop, and it was replaced in 1913 by the present shop building. In 1929, the Crandall Engineering Company of Boston designed and built a modern marine railway to replace the old block and tackle system of hauling boats for inspections and maintenance. It could accomplish in an hour a task that sometimes took up to three weeks to accomplish using the old skid ways. Unlike its predecessor, which was powered by fourteen horses, the new marine railway derived its power from two 150-hp steam engines.

# 2

The Shelburne Shipyard was already 116 years old when I first laid eyes on it one sunny summer day in June 1942. Only six months earlier the Aske family had been living in Minneapolis, after a move from Rockford, Illinois. It was in Rockford where, as an employee of the Hollibard and Root Company, Dad had been in charge of rebuilding Camp Grant, an old World War I Army facility. That project finished, he had taken a job with the Donovan Contracting Company of St. Paul, Minnesota, and we were living on Garfield Avenue, very close to one of the city's lakes. After church on the fateful Sunday morning of December 7, we called on a dear friend and former boss of Dad's—Clayton Griswold—who was dying of cancer. "Uncle Clayt" and "Auntie Kath" were like family. I think he was sort of a mentor when Dad was clerk of the works on a job at the University of Minnesota before going to Rockford. When we arrived at the door, Katherine ushered us upstairs to her husband's bedroom, and, even as an eight-year-old, I sensed that the hushed atmosphere signaled more than the seriousness of Clayt's condition.

He greeted me with the usual, "How you doin', skipper?" Then his tone turned very grave. I remember his exact words: "I guess you haven't heard. The Japs have just bombed Pearl Harbor."

While we were at church, the Griswolds had been listening to the radio and had heard the famous concert interruption. I asked my father what it all meant. Without hesitation he said that we would win the war, although it would be a long and diffi-cult task. At this point Congress had yet to declare war, but Dad figured we would be fighting not only the Japanese but Hitler's Germany and Mussolini's Italy as well. On one point he was absolutely certain—we would win in the end!

The very next morning my father and George Donovan sat down in his St. Paul office to discuss a new direction for the company. Up until this time, Donovan Con-tracting had been mainly engaged in rural electrification projects, and both men knew that this kind of work would be cut drastically *for the duration* (a phrase that was to become very familiar over the next four years). As a first step they would hire one of those companies that specialized in industrial matchmaking, the Roy B. Nelson Com-pany, to find a facility that could be converted to war production. Our family dinner talk for the next several days was almost exclusively about Dad's involvement with what now had become a United States war. His first inclination was to "sign up." He'd been too young to fight in the First World War and now, at age thirty-seven, he was probably too old to fight in the Second. This time, he felt he really needed to contribute in a major way to the war effort. In far-off Burlington, Vermont, his opportunity had been evolving since the previous summer.

Efforts to gain defense contracts were high priority for an area described in an editorial in the December 31, 1941 edition of the *Burlington Daily News* as "lagging far behind in this respect and which urgently needed them to boost the general prosperity." The previous April, the Navy Department had inspected the Shelburne Shipyard as a possible defense contracting facility. After being approved for naval shipbuilding and being invited to bid on 110-foot submarine chasers, the Shipyard's owners found themselves in the embarrassing position of being bankrupt under the rules of section 77B of the Federal Bankruptcy Act. The solution for their firm, the Champlain Transportation Company, as well as the greater Burlington area, would be a lease agreement with a strong and solvent company with which the Navy could do business.

On the seventeenth of December, 1941, the Nelson Company wired Horace Corbin, president of the Champlain Transportation Company:

> SEND PHOTO OR DRAWING OF PLANT LAYOUT **STOP** ADVISE TERMS OF
> LEASE AND NUMBER OF ONE HUNDRED FOOT WOOD SUBCHASERS POSSIBLE
> TO CONSTRUCT AT ONE TIME **STOP** ALSO WHETHER COMPLETELY EQUIPPED
> FOR THIS WORK **STOP** CLIENT RESPONSIBLE AND VERY MUCH INTERESTED

Although his grandfather Lars Aske had been a shipbuilder in Stevanger, Norway, who, with his brothers, had built a boat for the very purpose of migrating to the US, Dad had been born and raised in Moorhead, on Minnesota's northwestern border; his exposure to boats had been kayaks and canoes they shot ducks from on Little Pine Lake in Perham. Now he was about to become involved in the defense of his country as a shipbuilder. By the end of December he had personally checked out the Shipyard and scouted the area for potential subcontractors. He also had persuaded the directors of the local banks that it would be in the area's best interest for them to bail the Champlain Transportation Company out of bankruptcy, based upon Donovan's intent to lease the yard.

My mother and I saw little of my father that winter of 1942. After the lease was signed and the Shipyard was once again on the Navy's bidders' list, he went after the subchaser contract that had been lost due to the bankruptcy. His home was a room in the Hotel Vermont, on the corner of Main Street and St. Paul Street in Burlington, across from the Van Ness Hotel—which, incidentally, was named after one of the original owners of the Shelburne Shipyard property. Dad's tools were Western Union, a rather shopworn Corona portable typewriter and, on very special occasions, the

*Jerry Aske, Jr.*

One of the facilities on the Burlington waterfront that the Donovan Company's search team sent back to George Donovan as a possible shipbuilding site.

telephone (long distance being very expensive in those days). There was one additional tool: the Washingtonian/Montrealer train. His shuttles between Burlington, Vermont, and Washington, D.C. were to be regular occurrences throughout the war. In the space of three weeks following the signing of the lease he managed to reactivate the bid invitation from the Bureau of Shipbuilding (BUSHIPS), prepare a proposal and, on January 8, actually submit a firm, competitive bid. Now it was just a question of waiting for the Navy's reply.

Preparing and submitting the bid was only one of my father's tasks during late December and early January. He also had to assemble a work force in anticipation of a contract award. Although Vermonters were recognized as diligent, conscientious, and adaptable workers among New Englanders, those attributes, let alone the state itself, were hardly known around the rest of the nation. I recall a conversation back in Minneapolis, just before Dad left for the east, where a friend who had spent time in Vermont warned of the suspicious, tight-lipped nature of the native Vermonter. I will always remember his counsel, which was that while it is hard to break the ice with a Vermonter, if and when you do you can expect one hundred percent commitment. There were very few actual boat builders in the area, and many of the local carpenters had already left the state to look for work elsewhere. Dad's first hires were, by and large, farmers and 4-Fs—all that remained after enlistments and the draft had substantially reduced the Chittenden County work force. In fact, when one young man claimed to know absolutely nothing about boat building, but was willing to learn, my father hired him just on the basis of his honesty. Edward Bessette became an expert caulker ("corker") and remained with my dad until 1968. There were, to be sure, some older gentlemen with very special skills who came out of retirement to offer their help. Alex Terrien, cabinetmaker, and George Fortune, blacksmith, come to mind. In general, the new workforce was as new to boat building as my dad, who, at every break in his busy schedule, would study books on the subject. In fact when construction finally got under way, he would come home each day after work and cram for the next day in order to stay one step ahead of his novice crew.

Like any good defense plant, the Shelburne Shipyard would need security, too. I don't know how or where they met, but Chittenden County deputy sheriff Herb Ravlin was hired by my father to do whatever needed doing. Before long, there was a tall barbed-wire fence surrounding the entire property, a guardhouse at the entrance, and a signal-light station at the northeastern tip with line-of-sight to the Coast Guard station in Burlington. The idea behind the latter was that in the unlikely event of a communications breakdown, a visual S.O.S. could be sent to the nearest federal agency. Herb also took it upon himself to become the civilian equivalent of a British officer's batman. The man practically worshiped my dad, and I guess he was the first Vermonter to go that one hundred percent.

Things were moving pretty fast. The United States had entered the war on December 7, Dad had sent a bid on January 8, and now we were awaiting the Navy's response. Dad's calls and letters home were full of optimism, and I was looking forward to moving again. Moves were such a regular part of my life up to this point that more than a year in one place was a bore. Going to Vermont would be almost like migrating to another country. I was really excited. Then, from Washington on January 23, where he was monitoring the progress of the bid, Dad wired Burlington mayor John Burns:

NAVY HAS STATED AWARDS WILL BE ANNOUNCED MONDAY OR
TUESDAY **STOP** HAVE EVERY REASON TO BELIEVE OUR POSITION
SECURE BUT NOTHING CAN BE RELEASED FOR PUBLICATION NOW
**STOP** WILL ADVISE YOU MOMENT I HEAR.

After receiving such assurances from BUSHIPS, Dad was devastated when, on February 9, the Navy denied the contract on the grounds the Donovan Company was "not a bona fide shipbuilder…and… no contracts would be awarded in the future to

Observing George Donovan signing the lease for the Shipyard, 1942. (L to R): Mayor Burns, Horace Corbin, Dad, and Fred Fayette.

shipyards not now engaged in naval work." A man by the name of C.A. Jones, who worked for the Bureau of Ships, sent the following letter to the Honorable Charles A. Plumley, Vermont's lone representative to Congress:

> "The Bureau does not classify the Donovon [sic] company as a boat builder. In this connection, you will be interested to know that there exists in the country today more qualified boatbuilding companies, actually in operation, than are needed for the work of National Defense and for that of the country's Allies…It was because of this situation that the Bureau made the decision to permit only boat building companies, now in operation, to bid on the comparatively limited amount of work available…"

The Navy stated for the record that there were already enough shipyards currently active to serve the needs of the war effort. As incomprehensible as it now seems, this appeared to be the Navy's position in early 1942, when you would have thought that all potential war production facilities would have been sought after for mobilization.

My father wasn't about to give in so easily, however. Something just didn't seem right, and he enlisted help from other quarters. The Burlington Defense Industries Committee, spearheaded by Mayor John Burns and chaired by prominent automobile dealer Charles P. Smith, Jr., added its clout. Vermont Congressman Charles Plumley joined forces with Congressman Paul Kvale from Donovan's Minnesota district. With pressure being applied from many sides, evidence began to surface that suggested political interference was at the root of BUSHIPS' strange attitude. On February 20, Senator George D. Aiken wired the mayor that BUSHIPS had "reconsidered" and would award a contract to Donovan for construction of two 110-foot submarine chasers.

What actually had happened was that my father, frustrated with the run-around he was getting and unimpressed with the Bureau's feeble explanations, took a tip from a junior officer at the Navy Department and began sniffing around up on Capitol Hill. Satisfied that Congressman Plumley and Senator Aiken were firmly in his corner, he went to call on the senior member of the Vermont delegation, Senator Warren R. Austin. As recounted to my mother and me, after some initial sparring, Dad felt he was getting nowhere and started to leave—with a parting remark that maybe he could get better results from someone like fellow Minnesotan Westbrook Pegler (a muckraking columnist of the day). At this point the Senator admitted that it was *he* who had intervened and caused the Navy to renege on Donovan's contract but that he would now instruct the Navy to "reconsider." The outrageous reasoning behind Austin's action was that Vermonters did not like the idea of "outsiders" coming into their state and "wreaking havoc" with the local economy. Pressed further he said they felt the 40-cent-per-hour starting wage Donovan was offering was excessive for the Burlington area!

Another month passed and at last the contract was awarded and the keels were laid down (*1029* on April 27 and *1030* one week later). On April 29, 1942, Senator George D. Aiken drove the ceremonial first spike into the keel assembly of *SC 1029*. At my father's direction, and without any fanfare, something else was inserted into each keel that day: a Saint Christopher medal. At last the Shelburne Shipyard and the entire greater Burlington area were getting the economic boost that was so sorely needed.

# 3

The time finally had come for us to join Dad in Vermont. In June, as soon as the school year ended, Mother and I, her aunt Carrie, and Skippy, my cocker spaniel, headed east in our '41 Chrysler Windsor. Mother's cousin Ruth Anderson, her husband, Andy, and their son, Andy, Jr. (Bud), accompanied us in their '36 Ford V-8. A teacher by profession and an accomplished carpenter by avocation, Andy would work at the Shipyard until classes resumed in the fall. Without benefit of interstate highways and restricted by the newly imposed thirty-five MPH wartime speed limit, we pulled into the Haslam driveway in Barre, Vermont six days after leaving Minneapolis. Thelma Haslam, another of Mom's cousins, had moved to Vermont years earlier; her husband, Dan, had taken a job with the Rock of Ages granite company. Dad was there to greet us on that Saturday in June 1942. Bud, Pete Haslam, and I were about to begin a very memorable summer. The reunion party that evening was only a preview of the many, many more parties to come. Although these were serious times, folks did need some periods of recreation—and they were good at it!

We drove down to Shelburne the following Monday, and the first order of business after a quick tour of the shipyard was to find quarters for the Andersons and the Askes. The Andersons took rooms in Mr. and Mrs. Henry Tracy's spacious home in the village. After considerable searching, we finally found a three-bedroom apartment on the bay side of Shelburne Point, only a mile from the Shipyard. Dad's assistant manager, Jack Olson, and his wife, Peter, moved into the other downstairs apartment in the former manor house. The estate's caretakers and their families already occupied the two upstairs apartments. With a setting like this it was no wonder that, as word got around in Navy circles, Shelburne Shipyard received more than its share of "inspections" during the war. Ours was only a satellite facility for the Supervisor of Shipbuilding (SUPSHIPS) at the Bath Iron Works in Bath, Maine, but we attracted more brass than a yard of our size merited. After all, who could blame those commanders and captains for finding an excuse to get out of Washington? My folks and Petie and Jack Olson, assisted by the Andersons and the Haslams, were terrific hosts, and with the extra ration coupons allotted to defense contractors there was no shortage of steak and alcohol.

Not all the inspectors were high ranking. One unfortunate ensign probably wished he hadn't been so eager to inspect Shelburne. He came over from Bath in an official Navy carryall and on one off-duty evening, accompanied by a very *unofficial* local lady, he rolled it over on the sharp curve down by the present-day town beach.

Pete Haslam, me (with dogs), Dad at the helm, Thelma Haslam, and Mom aboard *Marjak*, summer 1942.

The Shelburne constable—a patriotic chap—brought the poor fellow back to our house where the party he had left was still in full swing. In the precious few hours remaining before he had to return to Bath, some shipyard employees and a generous soul from a local body shop tried to fix the dents and scrapes. Sadly, their efforts were in vain, because someone not-so-patriotic squealed to the Navy. Last we heard our ensign was on his way to the Pacific. More often than not, however, the higher-ranking officers who visited us came up from Washington using the same train my dad did—the Montrealer northbound and the Washingtonian going south.

Pete, Bud and I had adventures of our own to pursue. We were either in the lake or on it in my fourteen-foot Thompson rowboat. Propelled by a little three-and-a-half horsepower outboard motor dad bought brand new for $40 at Sears Roebuck, we explored most of the nearby coves and islands—even camping out overnight from time to time. We found we could gain entry to the steamboat *Vermont III* by pulling up under the empty paddlewheel box and climbing the ladder to the steel access hatch in the hull. Her machinery had been removed a few years earlier and sold for scrap and she was tied up at the dock that is now the main pier of my marina. Master shipwright Fred Barrett, his wife Ellen, and their son Luke lived in the house directly above the dock, where I now live. The first time we tried to board *Vermont III* in the conventional way, via the gangway, we got a tongue lashing from Ellen Barrett, who could best any Navy chief in that department. From then on we would sneak under the paddlebox and climb aboard that way. Though the machinery was missing, the steamboat was still very grand—a reminder of the kind of transportation Charles

*Jerry Aske, Jr.*

World War II crew of shipbuilders. Ed Bessette, front row, third from right. Armed guard Kieth Ravlin back row, far left.

Dickens had called "floating palaces" when he traveled the length of the lake in 1842. The first time I climbed the grand stairway from the cargo deck to the salon deck, I suddenly came face to face with someone coming down. Since we were under the impression that we were the only persons aboard, my heart stopped at this sudden apparition. It started again when I recognized that "someone"—it was my own reflection! *Chateaugay, Vermont III,* and *Ticonderoga* each had large mirrors mounted at the head of the grand staircase.

*Chateaugay*'s mirror ended up as a picture window in Corbin's, later my parent's, house. Today, re-silvered and once again a mirror, it is installed in the remodeled master bathroom. *Ticonderoga*'s, of course, is still aboard her at the Shelburne Museum. Sadly, *Vermont III*'s was destroyed along with most of her magnificent superstructure and appointments when she was converted to a freighter in 1945. Fred Barrett did salvage enough fixtures to install an indoor bathroom in his house, but most everything else went to the scrap heap. Actually, that conversion was to be the axis of a major turning point in my life.

Although we were far from the actual theaters of World War II, we did have the occasional close encounter—or so we thought—with the enemy. There was the time I was awakened in the middle of the night by the sounds of boat engines and commo-

Jack Olson and Dad inspect a shaft support assembly with a workman.

In the cruiser room. Back row (L to R): Dan Haslam Jr., Eddie Bessette, Fred Barrett, Rob Barrett, Cliff Martell, Ray Cootware, John Senesac. Front row (L to R): Jerry Aske, Jerry Aske Sr., Charlie Quinn, Donald Catella, and some of the shipyard workers.

*Jerry Aske, Jr.*

Rob Barrett and a helper at the forge.

tion on our beach. Not curious enough to get out of bed, I turned over and went back to sleep. The next day rumors were flying about a thwarted "Fifth Column" attack on the shipyard during the night. The noises I had heard were Coast Guard and Vermont Naval Volunteer patrol boats responding to a call from the shipyard. It seems one of the guards on duty that night, Herb Ravlin's son Keith, heard gunshots somewhere out on the water and was certain they were directed at him as he patrolled the Crandall railway. He dropped to the deck and began returning fire while his partner activated Herb's S.O.S. signal system and, for good measure, called the Coast Guard over the still-functioning landline. After a futile all-night effort, the patrols returned to base. Exaggerated stories about that night's close encounter with saboteurs circulated for weeks until, eventually, interest faded and the matter was forgotten. It would have remained that way forever had it not been for a chance meeting at Murph's Tavern one afternoon in the mid-1970s.

Sitting at our table was Shelburne native and Air Corps veteran George Lavallette. I was giving a history lesson to some of the younger guys who didn't know about the shipyard's involvement in World War II, and I had just finished with the "saboteur" story when Lavallette interrupted to tell us the rest of the story ...

That night in 1942 was a particularly hot and sticky one. George was home on his first furlough since a tour as a waist gunner aboard a B-17 bomber over Europe. What better way is there to cool off and relax than a night of walleye fishing on Shelburne Bay? If the fish weren't biting, there was always the option of attracting them with a flashlight and then blowing them out of the water with a gun. After several hours and several beers George and his fishing buddy were getting bored. The fish weren't biting and the light trick wasn't working. Knowing Keith Ravlin's propensity for overreaction they figured <u>he</u> would take the bait—hook, line and sinker! So they sneaked up close to shore, and when they saw him silhouetted in the moonlight at the end of the railway they squeezed off a couple of shots in his general direction and then "rowed like hell for open water." Ravlin's response hardly fazed Lavallette, who had grown accustomed to being shot at. Besides, by then he was well out of range. According to George, he and his buddy spent the rest of the night lurking along the shoreline, drinking their beer, and watching the Champlain Keystone Cops as they methodically checked oars and outboards for signs of recent use.

# 4

On August 31, 1942, the first two United States Naval vessels to be built on the shores of Lake Champlain since the War of 1812—*USS SC1029* and *USS SC1030*—were launched. It was also the first strictly double-launching in US Naval history, the two ships being side-by-side on the Crandall deck and floating off together. It even gained national attention. A picture of the unique event appeared in the September 1942 issue of *Yachting Magazine*. On August 28, Senator Warren Austin had wired to Jerry Aske, "Mrs. Austin and I will be pleased to attend launching August thirty-first. Kind regards, Warren R. Austin." He delivered the keynote address that day, praising the young men from Minnesota who had rescued the Burlington area from the Depression and the skilled Vermonters who had so readily adapted to the task of shipbuilding and had accomplished the job in record time.

On the launch platform along with the Senator that day were Fr. Francis Cain from Saint Catherine's Parish in Shelburne; Fr. Lyons, the president of Saint Michael's College; attorney Fred Fayette; Jack Olson and my father; assorted Navy brass, wives, and local dignitaries; and, of course, the ships' sponsors, Peter "Petie" Olson for *1030* and my mother for *1029*. Beneath the platform by the bow of *SC1029* I awaited the moment my mother would shout the time-honored phrase, "I christen thee...*USS SC 1029*," and break the bottle of champagne against the vessel's oak stem. I must have overly impressed my mother with the bad luck that befalls a ship whose sponsor needs more than one attempt to break the ribbon-encased bottle of bubbly. Traditionally, the ribbon and tape prevent the broken bottle from disintegrating altogether and it is later presented to the sponsor in a splendid mahogany case to display for posterity. After my mother's mighty swing there was little left to display except some unrecognizable wet ribbon and shards of glass hanging from the deck above. However, I did accomplish my goal: I wet my lips from the drippings.

The day was especially hot and humid, and once the ceremonies were concluded everyone set a course for the nearest trough. Jack Olson, a liquor salesman in civilian life, drew upon his expertise and arranged for one of the storage sheds to be set up as a beer and soft drink bar for the workers and their families and guests. The liquid selection at the VIP bar in the office complex was somewhat more generous.

The hulls now secured to the work dock, Dad was hosting his guests in this VIP area when he was summoned to join Senator Austin aboard Horace Corbin's yacht, *Chevela*, at an adjacent dock. Corbin had loaned her to Austin for the day, complete with a Filipino houseboy in a sailor suit. Dad followed the little sailor aft to the wait-

Keel-laying ceremony for *Subchaser (SC) 1029*, March 1942.

ing Senator, who was relaxing in a sumptuous rattan deck chair. As soon as he saw my father, he arose, extended his hand, and said, "Young man, let's let bygones be bygones," and with a toast to that sentiment, the hatchet was buried. Any questions the senator or the Navy may have had about awarding contracts to "shipyards not now engaged in Naval work" were no longer relevant.

This new confidence extended to our subcontractors as well. One Navy inspector compared the quality of the pilothouses that dad farmed out to the Haigh Lumber Company with what one would expect to find on a luxurious pleasure yacht. Coming from an old hand at wooden shipbuilding from Boothbay Harbor, Maine, this was an extraordinary complement. He was but one of several civilians with lifetimes of boat building experience that the Navy called out of retirement *for the duration*. It was clearly evident that my father's pledge to use Vermont labor and industry to the fullest had paid off.

Corbin later sold *Chevela* to Burlington businessmen Oskar and Walter Edlund, owners of the Edlund Can Opener Company. They, in turn, "loaned" it to the Coast Guard for submarine patrol duty in the Caribbean. This use of civilian craft for anti-submarine work was a stopgap measure until enough submarine chasers could be built to take over the job of protecting our vital coastal shipping lanes from German

SC 1029 and SC 1030 nearly ready for launching.

U-boats. Every sailor should recognize Oskar and Walter's last name since Edlund can openers were installed on practically every Navy ship afloat during World War II. As a matter of fact, they were in most shore installations of every branch of service as well. By the time the Coast Guard was finished with her, the boat had been abused to such a degree that the Edlunds didn't even bother to take her back. But she had helped avoid a near disaster along the Atlantic seaboard. By a strange coincidence, *Chevela* had been built in Germany.

Work began on three eighty-five-foot barges, called torpedo lighters, as soon as the Crandall railway was free. The subchasers would remain at the work dock for another couple of months before they would be ready for delivery. A month after the launching, *1029* was ready for an unofficial trial. With Shelburnite Earl Hedges at the engine room controls and Jack Olson handling the pilothouse telegraphs, she backed away from the work dock under her own power for the first time. Almost directly astern was one of the 35' x 35' timber cribs that were part of the old steamboat docking systems. Whether because of inexperience, nervousness, or both, the signals between Jack and Earl got mixed up and they rammed the crib hard enough to break off a large chunk of it. Repairs to the boat's transom would turn out to be just a little sanding and painting—another tribute to Vermont craftsmanship. The crib didn't fare as well, losing one whole corner to the mishap! But *1029's* trial was just beginning. Jack and Earl took her out on the broad lake and circled the Four Brothers Islands. Again, inexperience and carelessness put *1029* to another unnecessary test. They hit

August 31, 1942: The historic dual launching of first US warships on Lake Champlain since the War of 1812. Vermont Senator Warren R. Austin at microphone giving keynote address. Second and third from right: Dad and Jack Olson. Petie Olson at Austin's right, then Mother.

Dad looking on proudly as Mother gets ready to christen US *SC 1029* after Sen. Austin's speech.

*Jerry Aske, Jr.*

Petie Olson, sponsor of US *SC 1030*.

one of the reefs out there but fortunately only damaged one of the propellers.

Since these were the first naval vessels to come off the Shelburne ways, the Navy sent a star inspection team to conduct the official trials. Expecting to encounter relatively calm waters, these old hands were about to gain a healthy respect for Lake Champlain. As *1029* rounded the point and headed into the broad lake she plunged into a vicious chop churned up by a strong north wind. My father, the kayak skipper from Minnesota, had climbed into the crow's nest before they left the harbor. There he was forced to remain for the whole trial due to the severe pitching and rolling—a well-known subchaser characteristic, which was multiplied exponentially at the top of the mast! When they re-entered the harbor and he climbed back down to the flying bridge, he noticed a few "green gills" among the Navy people there. One of their older colleagues said, "Mr. Aske, any ship that can take a pounding like this can handle just about anything"—a prediction that was to prove even more accurate than he could have imagined at the time. Indeed, because of the short span between crests, seven- to eight-foot waves on Lake Champlain can be more punishing than thirty- or forty-foot swells on the ocean.

Arthur E. Allen, Jr., Lieutenant USNR, and a crew of enlisted men (some already combat veterans of the Pacific theater), arrived in Shelburne several weeks before the subchasers were ready for delivery. Allen and his crew had been assigned to *SC 1029*

*SC 1029* just inside the Burlington breakwater. Shelburne Point stands in the left background.

and, although she was not yet Navy property, he had volunteered to come to Shelburne and help with the fitting out in any way he could. This would be a great opportunity for him and his men to get to know their ship from stem to stern. To further help out and to get first-hand experience with his soon-to-be command, he offered to be our skipper for the delivery trip through the Champlain Canal and down the Hudson to the Brooklyn Navy Yard. Dad gladly accepted the offer. Rounding out the ship's complement for the delivery was the Reverend J. Lynwood "Lynn" Smith, pastor of Trinity Episcopal Church in Shelburne, and yours truly, two months short of my tenth birthday. In addition to his clerical vocation, Reverend Smith was an accomplished cabinetmaker (he later founded the Shelburne Craft School). In fact, he made the mahogany binnacle boxes for the ship's compasses. He and I were assigned to the double-deck berths in the wardroom that would later be occupied by Lieutenant Allen's two junior officers. Although they were unnamed, SCs were the smallest commissioned vessels in the US Navy, and *1029* was especially near and dear to my heart because my mother had christened her. *SC 1030* would follow with a Donovan crew, and steamboat captain Martin Fisher—on loan from the Champlain Transportation Company—at the helm.

*Jerry Aske, Jr.*

# 5

This was a once-in-a-lifetime experience for me. Even today, the smell of marine diesel evokes memories of that frosty November morning when I shipped off on 1029. My fifth grade teacher, Miss Noonan, heartily approved my absence provided I share my experiences with the class when I got back. I had been aboard 1029 many times—on the ways and at the dock—but now she was a ship come alive, all systems functioning, about to embark on a voyage into naval history. That first day we traveled to the head of the lake, securing for the night after locking up into the Champlain Canal at Whitehall, New York. It seemed like the whole town showed up to get a look at these United States warships, the first since Benedict Arnold built his Revolutionary War fleet there in 1776.

When you drive into Whitehall you are greeted by signs proclaiming it the "Birthplace of the United States Navy." Whitehall (known as Skenesboro in those days) can honestly lay claim to that title. Founded in 1759 by British army officer Philip Skene, it was captured in 1775 by an advance party of Ethan Allen's Green Mountain Boys as they prepared to attack Fort Ticonderoga. Had it not been for the gunboats produced there the following year we might still be flying the flag of St. Andrew instead of the Stars and Stripes. Winston Churchill wrote that the battle of Lake Champlain between the English and American fleets—though the colonials actually lost the engagement—was the turning point in the war for independence. Arnold's delaying action as he withdrew up the lake from Valcour Island and escaped to Fort Ticonderoga so upset the English commander's timetable that he retired back to Canada for the winter. This spared General Washington almost certain defeat had the English northern forces accomplished the planned link-up with their southern and western comrades.

Reverend Smith and I joined Lieutenant Allen and the crews of both ships at a popular Italian restaurant for a party hosted by the locals in Whitehall. We were all being entertained, but our Navy people were the toast of the town. After an enormous spaghetti dinner Lynn and I went back to the ship, but the party must have lasted well into the wee hours, judging from the number of obvious hangovers as we got under way the next morning. We transited the remaining twelve locks, securing for the night at the federal lock in Troy. I found plenty of diversions to occupy my time that day: learning to shoot craps in the fo'c'sle; losing a shoe when I caught my foot between the hull and a lock wall; watching gunnery practice. It was amusing, too, to see motorists' expressions as they stared down into the muzzles of two 20-mm

Oerlikon antiaircraft guns!

We were truly up close and personal with the many bridges that cross the canal; to pass safely beneath them not only the mast, but also everything on the flying bridge had been removed. It was helpful that the subchaser was so narrow. In fact, one of our helmsmen, a tall, lanky Texan who had just survived the sinking of his former ship—the aircraft carrier Hornet—as recently as October 27, remarked that this was the first time he'd ever "drove a ship where I could spit port and starboard and hit shore both ways!" This was not only my first trip on the canal; it was also my last at a speed of twelve knots: Because the canal is fairly narrow and the banks are vulnerable to erosion, there are strictly enforced speed limits during normal times. Due to our priority status we did not have to observe the speed limits. As I watched the shoreline crumbling in our big wake, I tried to picture the scene in earlier days when horses on towpaths "propelled" the canal boats. The Champlain Transportation Company's Captain Alanson Fisher had been a canal boat skipper in his youth, and his boats were towed by one or two horses. Now his son, Marty, was driving SC 1030 through the same waters propelled by two 1440 horsepower GM diesels. Unfortunately, as too often happens in wartime, little attention is paid to ecology. We probably did more damage in one day than those towpath-horses did during their entire history.

Our third day underway was fairly short but spectacular, with history and magnificent scenery around every bend of the upper Hudson. We passed through many towns during the last vestiges of autumn foliage: Schuylerville, one of many pre-railroad commercial ports along this important waterway; Bear Mountain, rising nearly vertically from the river; West Point and the United States Military Academy. To give my father time to fly down from Burlington and join us for the run into the Brooklyn Navy Yard, we tied up at a wharf in Yonkers—a maneuver that gave Lieutenant Allen his first taste of 1029's responsiveness. Approaching the pier from upriver, he ordered the engines to back one-third. With the combined normal current and an outgoing tide we were still closing too fast. Even to this day I am impressed by the young skipper's composure as he calmly ordered, "All engines back, full," and the sailor at the telegraph just as routinely sent the signal to the engine room. Men on the dock, waiting to take our lines, were beginning to scatter when, effortlessly, our ship slowed and with the final commands, "Port stop, starboard back two-thirds, full right rudder," our port side nested comfortably against the pier. Marty brought 1030 in behind us without any trouble. I'm sure his years of piloting sidewheel steamboats factored into his easy landing, but I also believe he shrewdly observed Art's landing and adjusted accordingly.

Sharing the pier with us was a launch from the Swedish oceanliner Gripsholm. She was chartered to the US State Department as a repatriation and exchange ship.

My father-in-law, Admiral John Roper, in his Shelburne-built "Captain's Gig." His flag at bow signifies he's aboard.

She had been anchored in mid-channel since August 25 after her first exchange voyage, which lasted nearly three months. She had left with a "cargo" of mostly Japanese nationals and returned with Westerners who had been interned by the Japanese. Following a nine-month layover in Yonkers—where her Swedish crew was accorded the same privileges as US servicemen on leave—Gripsholm made eleven more exchange trips all around the world.

Reverend Smith, Jack Olson, and I took the train into New York City where we met my dad, who had come down for the actual delivery; we all joined the ship for the final leg of the trip. That day I saw the George Washington Bridge for the first time—from underneath. Cruising further down the Manhattan side of the river we passed the oceanliner piers where so many gala arrivals and departures used to occur. I was daydreaming about the happy times—people on the docks waving and yelling to friends and relatives on board as confetti and band music filled the air—when Normandie hove into view. There, alongside pier 88, lay the capsized, burnt-out hulk of a once proud queen of French liners. When France surrendered to Nazi Germany in June of 1940, Normandie was in New York, her transatlantic runs already having been suspended because of the impending war in Europe. Since France had surrendered to Germany, our Coast Guard took her into protective custody, and after we became combatants against the Vichy French government, the Tricolor flag was hauled down and the Stars and Stripes hoisted as the US Navy took Normandie as a prize of war. Lacking a drydock large enough for her conversion to a troop transport, work was begun at the pier. As her conversion was nearing completion a welder's spark started a fire that, although small at first, grew out of control due to a series of stupid mistakes. Finally, the water being pumped into her upper decks rendered her top heavy and she rolled over onto her port side. She would never sail again and was a very sorry sight, indeed.

My spirits rose, though, when we rounded the battery and I caught my first glimpse of the Statue of Liberty. Then, as we passed under the Brooklyn Bridge, we were followed by a US warship, seriously wounded but with colors flying and band playing. I knew she would soon be back in action against our enemies. On the ways at the Navy Yard was the nearly completed battleship New Jersey, BB 63, and across from our slip lay some PT boats. By an uncanny coincidence, shortly after the war, my future father-in-law, John W. Roper, hoisted his flag aboard New Jersey as his flagship when he was commander of Battleship Division One—including Iowa, New Jersey, and Wisconsin. All were soon to give our enemies some major discomfort. I felt pretty good again. My optimism about the outcome returned. Dad was right: We would win in the end.

I watched a comical episode unfold with one of the PT boats nearest us. A young officer boarded one of the boats; as viewed from our ship, he appeared to be the new commanding officer. Some of the crew were busy attending to routine chores, mopping and painting and generally just making things shipshape. Our young hero, after a brief conversation with one of his petty officers, climbed into the driver's seat and soon those powerful airplane engines roared to life. Presumably by his orders dock lines were cast off and we can only assume he rang full speed ahead because the boat leaped away from the dock leaving mops, buckets, paint cans and a few sailors bobbing in her wake! Might that ensign's name have been Kennedy?

Arriving at the Navy Yard, our job was finished. Dad officially turned the ships over to the United Sates Navy on November 16, 1942 and Lieutenant Allen officially became the captain of USS SC1029. He wrote to dad on January 19, 1943:

U.S.S. SC – 1029
c/o Postmaster
New York, New York
January 19, 1943

Dear Jerry,

We were very pleased when we caught up with three weeks' mail to find a check from the Donovan Contracting Company for the ship's welfare fund and I can assure you that all hands appreciate this Christmas present very much. We have not as yet invested the money in any specific items but a bicycle, fishing tackle, and other athletic equipment will, I think, shortly appear through your generosity.

You will be interested to know that we have had an opportunity to see how the 1029 would act under adverse conditions and I might say that the splendid way in which she performed was a real tribute to the honest and conscientious workmanship that went into her building. Mr. Donovan, you, and Jack. Olsen [sic], together with all of your shipyard crew can well take pride in the job you did on this ship. I wish that some of your men who thought that the first trial run in the lake was rough water could have spent two days in a full gale as we did recently. It would have been an eye-opener for them. However, there were no casualties except for two broken ribs suffered by one of the crew.

We have had considerable changes in the personnel and I now have two new officers with me together with a number of new crew members. The crew has been enlarged to twenty-four from the former twenty. All of those who were in Burlington, however, with the exception of the Boatswain Mate, Machinist Mate, and the Signalman, are still on board.

Please send my best wishes, together with those of the crew, to Mr. Donovan, Mr. and Mrs. Olson, Mrs. Aske and yourself and to all of the men who contributed to the making of the 1029 the stout ship which she is.

Sincerely yours,
(signed)
Arthur E. Allen Jr.

(And a hand written postscript) Chief Smith joins particularly in sending his best wishes.

This communiqué was probably written while 1029 was in the Caribbean on submarine patrol. German U-boats were lurking about in our territorial waters and sinking coastal cargo ships on a regular basis, often within sight of shore. Subchasers were our only defense against these bold aggressors, the rest of our navy being either at the bottom of Pear Harbor or so occupied with the Atlantic and Pacific theaters of war that no ships could be spared to defend our own coastline. Lynn Smith received a letter from Allen some time later:

> The 1029 is still going strong and has piled up a pretty nice record. After spending the winter convoying in the Caribbean where I eventually became commander of a task unit of five SCs, we left in March and after getting additional equipment, formed part of the escort for a large convoy to the Mediterranean. We were in the last part of the Tunisian campaign and then in the Sicilian invasion where we were one of the first (as far as I know the first) ships off Sicily. From then on we were based in a large Northern Sicilian port and since the campaign the 1029 has been busy between Italy, Sicily, and Africa. So far she has been very lucky, her closest shave coming one night when we were dive-bombed and two of the men were blown violently down the hatch by the concussion from a near miss. The 1029, I'm proud to say, has the finest efficiency record in the Mediterranean and I believe shows the largest number of hours of operation of any ship in our Navy there.

More recently, Art Cohn, executive director of the Lake Champlain Maritime Museum, interviewed both of Lieutenant Allen's junior officers as well as one of the enlisted crew. He learned that the "dive-bombing" incident that Allen relayed to Revered Smith actually resulted in the death of a Navy man from, of all places, Vermont. Anthony Sankowski from West Rutland died of shrapnel wounds during the incident. In an article printed in the June 6, 2005 edition of the Rutland Herald newspaper, reporter Wilson Ring wrote,

> It was only recently that Sankowski's relatives learned that the SC1029 he served on was built at the Shelburne Shipyard, was crafted from oak trees harvested in Ferrisburgh and that it did its sea trials on Lake Champlain.
> Five sub chasers were built in Shelburne, but only two, the 1029 and 1030, made it to Europe.
> Art Cohn [of the Lake Champlain Maritime Museum] said a former commanding officer of the SC1029 [Lt. Allen] told him that the Ferrisburgh white oak is what saved the vessel from sinking after the explosion

*Jerry Aske, Jr.*

that killed Anthony Sankowski and another sailor. The original design called for yellow pine [planking], which wouldn't have weathered the blast.

"When that explosive charge went off, any other boat would have been destroyed ... I want you to know, this subchaser was probably the best sub chaser ever built for the Navy," Cohn quoted the former commander as saying. "We were very proud of this boat. It was built by true craftsmen."

Once again, my father's determination to buy locally had paid off. As Art Cohn found out, if it had not been for the change order requested by my dad and approved by BUSHIPS,1029 would have been planked with pine instead of oak. The reason for the order change was that it was nearly impossible to purchase clear Southern yellow pine at any price, demand being so great, and "just down the road a-piece" was an abundant supply of oak waiting to be cut and milled. The only casualty suffered by any of the shipyard crew during the war happened while harvesting some of this timber. Bernard Coleman, a native of Shelburne, peered over a log barrier to see the explosion as the Gebo lumberjacks were dynamiting some tree stumps. His curiosity cost him an eye!

Regarding SC 1030, I remember seeing a postcard (presumably no longer extant) from Art Allen to Lynn Smith where he gave glowing reports about 1029's performance and then said, "sister, I'm afraid, didn't fare so well." Whether this meant 1030 was sunk or just had some tough luck we never knew until recently, when I read the excellent book about subchasers, Splinter Fleet, by Ted Treadwell. In chapter six, Treadwell records 1030 as being part of the southern France invasion force and later being turned over to the French on October 2, 1944 as CH-136 (fate unknown). My dear 1029 was also listed as CH-123 on October 30, 1944, and was struck from the Navy Register on August 12, 1953. Treadewell also describes an earlier collision, which I suspect is the mishap Allen referred to in his postcard: 1030 was rammed amidships by a PC off Sicily's southwest coast in July of 1943. We know both Shelburne boats were there for the Sicilian campaign and, if memory serves me correctly, the postcard was sent from a just-liberated Rome where Allen was sightseeing. The fact that she didn't sink and lived to fight again is probably another example of the virtues of Vermont white oak versus Southern yellow pine. Maybe, too, those Saint Christopher medals helped a little bit! Our other three SCs were given to the Soviet Union under the Lend-Lease program, although there is some question as to whether the Soviets received all of them. At least one may have been lost when its convoy to Murmansk was shattered by a fierce hurricane.

# 6

Meanwhile, as we celebrated the delivery of *1029* and *1030*, work on the three torpedo lighters had to be finished so they could be towed through the Champlain Canal before it froze. To speed construction my father decided to build them upside down (a technique he was to use again in the 1950s to build landing craft for the Navy). While this certainly simplified construction, especially when it came to bottom planking and caulking, he didn't foresee how difficult it would be to right those scows after they were launched. A-frames had been erected on each bottom, and the plan was to turn the hull over by securing a gunwale to the shore and running a line from the A-frame to a tugboat. Good plan. But my father hadn't taken into account the tremendous suction that would be resisting the flip. After many failed attempts, and several parted hawsers, he ordered the men to chop holes in the bottoms to relieve the suction. This was not a glamorous launching, but truly there was nothing glamorous about these new additions to Uncle Sam's navy. After a hurried haul-out to patch the holes, the torpedo lighter barges were towed to another work dock across the slip from the subchasers, which were at that point nearly ready to depart.

As there was minimal post launch work to be done, the barges were ready for their trip south by early December. But when they reached the narrow headwaters of the lake and began to encounter ice, our tugboat, *Pocahontas,* had to return to the yard so her stem and bow planking could be reinforced with steel plate. Winter came early that year. Shelburne Bay already had frozen over the night before my parents and I were driven to the Shelburne train station (now in the Shelburne Museum) where we waited and shivered until the Rutland Railroad's train to Troy, New York, arrived. This was the first leg of our trip back to Minnesota for Christmas. The Twentieth Century Limited from Albany to Chicago was overflowing with servicemen and Dad invited one of them to sleep on the floor of our compartment. The train from Minneapolis to Moorhead was made up of cars that had been resurrected from the boneyard in an effort to meet the wartime needs. The only heat came from small coal stoves at each end, and the outside temperature was way below zero. Some of the soldiers were forced to stand in the areas between the cars, where there was no heat at all. It was on this train that I was entertained by a gregarious character named Douglas Leigh. He amused me with a new "invention" of his—a little wire loop and a jar of soapy water. His soap bubbles were far superior to the ones I used to make with a pipe. Later he became famous for his smoke ring billboard in Times Square.

Two of four yard tug (YT) boats framed and ready for planking.

Despite the difficulties, the barges finally broke through to the open waters of the Hudson. A three-man crew, with chief Ravlin in charge, lived aboard the last barge in a crude frame-and-canvas structure for nearly two months. Christmas Day found this unlikely trio of rural Vermonters taking in the sights along the Great White Way (severely dimmed because of wartime precautions) while waiting for a seagoing Moran tug to take them the rest of the way to Norfolk, Virginia. As Herb recounted it, Ken Coleman and Ed Bessette were dressed like they had just come down from deer camp—felt boots, ear-lappers and all. They must have presented quite a sight to the clerk at Schrafft's Fifth Avenue candy shop. Showing no sign of embarrassment and apparently unconcerned about cost, Eddie made his selection; when the girl began to carefully place each piece of chocolate in its own little paper cup he said, "Never mind them things. Just fill up the sack."

What these two may have lacked in sophistication they more than made up for in loyalty. Two other men who had begun the voyage had long since abandoned ship. New Year's Day found the trio on the high seas, decks covered with ice, and only a potbellied wood stove for heat. When riding in beam seas, far behind their tug, the large swells would roll the barge back and forth, port and starboard, over and over again. At times like these the stove would break free and disengage from the stove-

Jack Olson, in coat and tie, at stern of nearly completed yard tug on Crandall railway.

pipe, and the tent would be engulfed in smoke. Ever resourceful, Eddie would sit to one side while Ken sat opposite. Each time the pipe came loose one man would kick the stove back and the other would pop the pipe on again. And while they were definitely loyal they were very upset when Herb insisted they shave before entering the Navy base. The last day out they finally gave in. Just as they finished cutting off their scruffy whiskers, a submarine surfaced nearby. Out of the hatches scrambled several of our Navy's elite—all sporting very impressive, war-patrol beards! Despite all the difficulties the torpedo lighters delivery was accomplished on schedule.

The next successful bid my father submitted was for the construction of four 66-foot yard tugs, called YTs. They were part of an order for thirty that the Navy had placed with BUSHIPS. Since much of the lumber earmarked for these boats was located in Pennsylvania, Dad decided to save shipping costs and avoid possible delays by once again using Vermont oak from the Gebo mill in Ferrisburgh. Gebo's foreman, Leroy "Red" Plumber, remembered helping to select the best oak from that area and skidding the logs to the mill, sometimes with horses when the terrain was impassable for the Caterpillar tractor.

Dad's own people roamed the woods of Ferrisburgh and vicinity selecting trees for keels and ribs. The former required trees at least forty-five feet in length, and they

Launching day for four yard tugs (YTs)—not as fancy as the Subchasers, but still drawing a crowded audience.

*Jerry Aske, Jr.*

had to be clear and straight. Finally, the oaks were felled and hauled to the mill where they were sawed into timbers. The stock was then trucked to the shipyard for on-site cutting and shaping.

Due to wartime shortages, hardware that would usually be available through normal channels was often unobtainable. Items like bilge pump strainers—similar to sink traps but a lot bigger—were on 120-day backorder. So my dad again turned to Vermont talent. Local welders would fabricate them from scratch. Propeller shafts were turned from rough castings on an old lathe that the Stevens Machine Shop in Winooski returned to service specifically for this job. It may have been old, but it had the requisite twenty-foot bed. Fuel tanks were fabricated by the Vermont Structural Steel Company of Burlington. Spin-off bonuses for this subcontractor were orders from shipyards that were building twenty-six other YTs, much to owner Floyd "Dinty" Moore's unanticipated delight. And T. Arnold Haigh's lumber company continued to manufacture cabins, hatches, and other cabinetry. The yard tug project became an almost all-Vermont undertaking.

With the tugs' launching scheduled for mid-April with delivery as soon as the ice went out of the canal in May, Dad started planning ahead. In early March he headed back to Washington, D.C. to drum up more work from BUSHIPS. He could now proudly boast that, in addition to the outstanding record of performance on two submarine chasers and three torpedo lighters, the four yard tugboats nearing completion were made from Vermont lumber by a nearly 100 percent Vermont workforce. And all in less than a year since the first contract had been awarded.

Then the unthinkable occurred. On April 8, the *Burlington Daily News* was announcing in two lines of inch-and-a-quarter type: "SHELBURNE YARDS MAY CLOSE; 165 SHIPBUILDERS FACE LAY-OFF." The sub-headlines were likewise damaging: "Lack of Contracts May Force Shutdown of Important Industries"; "Aske Seeking Order for More Wooden Boats"; "Navy isn't Calling for Wooden Craft; Donovan Company Cancels its Lease." In the follow-up article, the *Daily News'* Harry Holden reported:

> Splendid cooperation was reported from Washington authorities because of the clean-cut record of the Donovan firm in the building of the two subchasers and the three torpedo lighters and the progress made on the four tugs. But the Navy now has a policy of not building any more wooden boats of size such as will pass through the Champlain Canal to the Hudson River and thence to the Atlantic…Some hope for more orders…was held today in wake of an announcement that President Roosevelt was asking for some 25 billion dollars for the Navy.

Yard tugs launched into an icy Lake Champlain.

Whatever had happened, the fact is that Donovan did not cancel the lease and they did receive one more contract, this time for three more 110-foot subchasers, *SC1504, SC1505,* and *SC1506.* They were specially fitted out for cold weather operations and scheduled for delivery to the Soviet Union under the Lend-Lease program. In the late 1950s I met a former naval officer who had been in a convoy heading for the Soviet port of Murmansk. He was quite certain that at least one of those numbers were among the list of ships lost in a severe North Atlantic storm.

This time the Crandall Railway was needed by the Champlain Transportation Company in order to service some of its ferryboats, so my father had the Rutland Railroad construct a standard gauge railroad track down into the water. The three SCs were built on cradles equipped with regular railcar wheels and a "head house" was set up with a gasoline engine and tackle so the boats could be lowered into the lake. Unfortunately, Dad was not to be present for these launchings.

Towards the middle of this contract, Dad and George Donovan quarreled over who had authority at Shelburne. From the outset of their relationship Donovan seemed uncomfortable with giving too much control to someone so far from the home office in St. Paul. Donovan's longtime friend, Jack Olson, was sent to Shelburne with the title of Assistant Manager. My father always suspected that Jack was really

*Jerry Aske, Jr.*

sent for another, more devious purpose, namely, to be Donovan's eyes and ears at his Vermont facility. After all, this amiable liquor salesman had no engineering experience whatsoever. And, in fact, Jerry and Virginia Aske and Jack and Petie Olson became very close friends and I am sure Jack never sent an adverse report back to St. Paul. As I look back on those days I think that Olson's decision to leave the company and become a "ninety-day wonder" naval officer soon after completion of the last subchaser job was prompted by distaste for his mission from Donovan. He had come to know my father as a man of unquestionable integrity and loyalty.

Olson's replacement was a character of a different sort. After several months of interference by this new "spy," an exasperated Jerry Aske phoned George Donovan in St. Paul. I was in the room and heard Dad's end of the conversation. It was not friendly; he quit. In a way I was kind of excited. We'd been moving every year or two for as long as I could remember. Now we would be going home to Minnesota. But our move would have to wait ... Dad was offered a job at the Bell Aircraft plant in Burlington. He would remain there *for the duration*.

# 7

Early fall, 1945—VJ Day! The War was over! But my long anticipated return to Minnesota had already been scuttled when Horace Corbin asked Dad to supervise the conversion of *Vermont III* into a freighter, contrary to the statement on page 67 of the Shelburne Museum book, *Ticonderoga*, that claims, "*Vermont III*, unused since 1932, was dismantled in 1943-44." To the best of my recollection, dad's new job, which became another life changer for me, actually took place in 1945. The photograph by L. L. McAllister on page 67 of the same book was not taken "at the Burlington waterfront," but at the Shelburne Shipyard next to the Crandall Railway shortly after *Vermont III* was unceremoniously stripped of her superstructure, hauled out of the water for installation of a shaft and propeller, and re-launched for her trial run.

What they did to that magnificent ship still upsets me. Her machinery had long since been removed and sold for scrap, and at the time preserving an old boat like this wasn't even a remote consideration. In fact, Corbin had been trying to get rid of the ship for years. The following exchange of letters between him and my father attest to this fact.

Burlington, Vt.
February 10, 1942

Mr. L. J. Aske
Donovan Contracting Co.
1725 Carroll Ave.
St. Paul, Minn.

Dear Mr. Aske:

I was very glad to receive your encouraging letter of the 5th because it contradicts one which was published in the local paper which stated there was a shortage of boat orders now for the existing yards and furthermore that Donovan could not receive the contract owing to the fact that he was not a shipbuilder. This was supposed to have been sent to the Mayor by Representative Plumley.

I am enclosing a clipping from the Baltimore Sun and have just returned from checking this with a party in New York and there is no question but what we can put the *Vermont* in position to meet the requirements for this ferry service. If you will look in the "Maritime Report" of January 29th … you will note that the *Chateaugay* is going to be reconstructed and equipped with diesel engines for the Electric Ferries, Inc. This is the vessel that was fifty-five years old that we cut in slices and took up to Lake Winnipesaukee where she was rewelded and put in operation with a steam plant. Now to remove her from the lake the Electric Ferries, Inc. or the General Ship and Engine Co. must again cut her in sections, put her on a train and take her to Boston. Here we have the "Vermont" which was built sixteen years later of much stronger material, that can be floated right out of the lake and taken directly down to New York. If you can come up to Burlington I can show you definite proof that the states of Michigan, Maryland, Texas, Florida, Virginia and Washington are all in the market for ferry boats to take labor back and forth to their shipyards, etc. As I explained to you, this boat can be purchased from The Champlain Transportation Company, fitted with the engines (if they have not been sold) from Washington that we discussed and work could be started on this project at once. I am enclosing a copy of the construction of the hull of the *Vermont* which is far and above any standards today of marine construction. At that time the D. & H. Railroad owned this company and they spared no expense in the construction of this hull and no matter what boat anyone buys or builds, it has got to be started with a hull.

If this interests your organization in any way, please advise me by wire as I feel we both have an interest in this organization and we could really go along together and make some money. However, if you are not interested in this, please advise so that I can complete arrangements with other parties.

Here's hoping you get contracts and in the event you do take the yard over, then the *Vermont* parties would either have to reconstruct her in some other yard or meet your terms provided we do not make arrangements prior to the completion of your lease.

Kind personal regards to you both and best of luck.

> Sincerely,
> (signed)
> H. W. Corbin
> General Manager

*Jerry Aske, Jr.*

And my father's reply:

Mr. H. W. Corbin
Champlain Transportation Company
Burlington, Vermont

Dear Mr. Corbin:

We have your letter of February 10th on the *Vermont* matter and it does seem that there should be a chance to do something with this vessel if the *Chateaugay* can be cut up again, shipped overland and be reassembled at a profit.

We are interested in this and Mr. Donovan agrees that if you can find a market for the converted boat showing the right kind of profit, he will go into the deal with you. It does not seem, however, that it should be necessary for either of us to make a trip to Burlington at this time.

If this is to be a profit sharing enterprise, as we understand that it is, we feel that you should find a buyer and submit a profit estimate to us. If the earnings look right we will then finance the undertaking as purchaser of the boat from the present owner, and handle the cost of conversion including purchase of new engines. You are in a much better position to find a buyer than we are and we feel that this should be a part of your contribution to the enterprise.

We presume that you have received our letter of the 11th with reference to the Navy shipbuilding deal. We sincerely hope that something can be done to change the Navy policy and enable us to proceed with our original plans for Shelbourne [sic] Harbor.

If it develops, however, that we do not operate the shipyard, we could still handle the *Vermont* deal paying the present owners of the yard for the work of converting the boat.

Very truly yours,
DONOVAN CONTRACTING CO.
By (signed L. J. Aske)

The *Vermont III* just before its demolition.

Author Ralph Nading Hill, who later spearheaded the successful effort to save the *Ticonderoga*, Herb Ravlin, and I were aboard what was left of *Vermont III* when she was taken out for her first trials. Now driven by a propeller, and minus all her superstructure, she broached immediately after we left the relative calm of the harbor. Without steerage, we drifted helplessly until the yard sent the tug *General Allen* to our rescue. Ballasting her bilges with seawater ultimately solved the steering problem. Eventually she was seaworthy enough to leave the lake and take up new duties as a coastal banana boat until she caught fire and sank somewhere upriver in the Southeast. With *Vermont*'s inglorious demise only *Ticonderoga* remained as a reminder of those bygone days of Dickens' "floating palaces."

Late Fall, 1945. Finally we're going back home to Minnesota! Except … enter Horace Corbin again. This time with a proposal to sell the shipyard to us, with a juicy contract thrown into the bargain—the construction of a brand new ferryboat for his Champlain Transportation Company. I think this was when the three of us realized how much a part of Shelburne we had become. I had entered the fifth grade there and was now starting my second year in junior high. All Shelburne's classes, from first grade through high school, were held in the same building, then called "Shelburne

*Vermont III* at its winter dock, which is now an anchor for the marina.

High"; today the building houses the Shelburne town offices. Mom and Dad had made many close friends in the Shelburne/Burlington community. The more we talked about it the more enticing Corbin's offer became. Thus, on January 1, 1946, after one hundred thirteen years of ownership by the Champlain Transportation Company, the Shelburne Shipyard passed to Jerry Aske, Sr., and his younger brother Wendell, under the umbrella of their newly charted corporation, Shelburne Harbor Ship and Marine Construction Company, Inc. To pull it off they had needed some financial help and this came from their father—my Grandpa Aske, who remarked to me how great it was that our shipbuilding heritage, having bypassed one generation, had now been resurrected in his sons.

As soon as their furniture arrived from Minnesota, Wendell and my Aunt Elynor moved into the lake end of the apartment house, or "block" as it was known to the old shipyard hands. During the *Vermont III* conversion, her new owners, the Reynolds brothers from Georgia, had lived there and thanks to them the three little privies out back had been replaced with indoor plumbing. We moved from our wartime apartment (now the Eastlake condominiums) to the "big house," originally built for the CT Company's senior captain, John Rushlow. It, too, had indoor plumbing. At

Tugboat *General Allen* to the rescue! Ralph Hill (center) and me (left) on foredeck of *Vermont III*. Minus her superstructure, *Vermont* was unmaneouverable.

that time we did not own the shipyard's residential properties, but leased our new quarters (and Wendell's) from Corbin. In some respects, the shipyard seemed to be stepping back into its steamboat days. The boarding house was reactivated to accommodate the scores of expert welders Dad imported from the Boston area.

Attached to the garage was a stable Corbin had had built for his daughter, Lorraine, when they lived there before the war; my grandfather, believing that every boy should have a horse, bought "Blackie" for me. One of the welders' wives was hired to handle the kitchen duties and her daughter fell in love with my horse, which was fine with me because she volunteered to handle Blackie's early morning feeding. When my Minnesota cousin Tom Cairns spent the summer of 1947 with me, we used to borrow one of Harry Webb's old workhorses from the north pasture so we could ride together. This old nag was so big that the cinch on my extra saddle barely reached around her belly. We mostly occupied the sleeping porch at the northwest corner of the house, but occasionally slept aboard *Pocahontas,* which was tied up at the recently vacated *Vermont III* pier. We didn't need alarm clocks that summer with all the diesel welding generators and chipping hammers starting up on the nearly completed all-welded steel ferryboat, *Valcour,* every morning at seven o'clock! We were aboard later

*Jerry Aske, Jr.*

Aircraft carrier-style pilot house kept *Valcour's* decks clear for large trucks.

that summer when she was unceremoniously floated off the Crandall. No fanfare like the August 31 launching in 1942 for *1029* and *1030*!

Work had begun on *Valcour* soon after we purchased the yard. I remember riding with our tractor-trailer driver that spring when we were bringing steel from the Shelburne railroad station to the yard. Because there were still wartime shortages, all the steel for the new ferry was government surplus flat plate of varying thickness. Every angle, channel, and other shape that normally would be purchased in final form was cut, welded, and otherwise fabricated right there at the shipyard. As is usual in Vermont during springtime, it rained a lot that year. Driving a ten-wheeler loaded down with iron back and forth over an unpaved Harbor Road gave new meaning to the term "mud season!"

Just like the steel plate, the engines were also government surplus, and they were far too heavy to transport from the railroad by truck. Later that summer of 1947, Tom and I were once again aboard when *Valcour* was towed over to Burlington where a railroad crane transferred the four engines from the railroad cars to the boat. As originally built she had two complete engine rooms with a pair of Clark four-cylinder direct reversible engines in each one. *Valcour* was unique in another respect in that

One of Valcour's two identical engine rooms.

her pilothouse was mounted off to the side, like an aircraft carrier, so she could accommodate trucks of any height. There were two separate helms—one at each end. The only differentiation between port and starboard was her running lights. She also had her own Saint Christopher medal, pounded into a crack in the pilothouse by yours truly.

Another job for our new company was conversion of the old Riker's Island ferryboat *Mott Haven* into a flattop. With all that weight on one side of the boat she had a distinct list. I have to take credit for solving that problem. My dad took my suggestion that they fill the opposite bulwarks with concrete. It worked! *Mott Haven* was to share the Burlington-Port Kent run with *Valcour* until she was sold in 1961. We also built the 63-foot yacht *Franny Bee* for Mr. Arthur Broughton of Glens Falls, New York, and a 38-foot cruiser for a Mr. Ed Ives with the proviso that he would relinquish his rights to its design and we could mass-produce it as a stock pleasure boat to be called the "Shelburne 38." With our fleet of three tugboats and a steam-operated lighter we supplemented boat construction with other marine work, such as repairing the Burlington breakwater and driving pilings for the ferryboat slips.

An unexpected bonus accompanied the delivery of *Valcour* to Corbin. There were performance incentives written into the contract as well as potential penalties. Halfway through the job my father became dissatisfied with the pace of construction

*Jerry Aske, Jr.*

Custom yacht *Franny Bee* just after launching.

and he fired the supervisor whom Corbin had recommended. From that point he took on the supervisory task himself. I think he wore out every one of his dress shoes on those steel decks, and suffered temporary blindness from welding flashes, among other things, but the boat was finished ahead of schedule. The upshot was that, as part of the performance reward, we acquired the rest of the shipyard properties. For the first time in my life, I was living in a home that actually belonged to us!

Now that we were bona fide Shelburne property owners and taxpayers, my father and Wendell thought it would be okay for them to take part in the democratic process called town meeting. Never mind that my dad had resided in Shelburne since 1942 and had never been so presumptuous as to involve himself in local politics. After all, he had always planned on remaining in Vermont only *for the duration.* At any rate, they quietly took their seats in the town hall and basically listened to the give and take so typical of these annual Vermont meetings until, at one point, my dad rose to ask a simple question relating to one of the warnings to be voted on. In those days we students were excused from classes so we could go over to the town hall and watch democracy in progress; I remember my dad asking his question, which simply was for an explanation of an item he did not understand. Barely into his query, Mrs. Eustace "Rita Mom" Thomas waved her hand and was recognized by the moderator. "Yes, Rita Mom," said Dr. Norton, brushing cigarette ashes from his dark blue suit. "Mister

Moderator, I don't think Mr. Aske has lived here long enough to be asking questions in our town meetin." Whereupon Dr. Norton, the local country doctor as well as town moderator, banged his gavel (actually a medical reflex tool) and declared, "I agree. Mr. Aske is out of order."

So my dad sat down and remained silent for another three or four years. Such were the wonderful local politics of those days. Eventually, Rita Mom Thomas became one of those Vermonters to grant us the 100 percent acceptance. "Newcomer" Virginia Aske became the organist at Saint Catherine's church when her dear friend and predecessor Mrs. Thomas died. Gradually, we were accepted into the community. Not long thereafter my uncle was elected to the board of selectmen and years later he was appointed Shelburne's first town manager.

The new business was doing quite well, despite the loss of our three tugboats and lighter to the 1949 Thanksgiving hurricane. We even had a fling at designing and building mobile homes. And then, on June 25, 1950, the Korean War began. It was back to government work—completing the circle of employment. This time, because of the record achieved during World War II (including the Army/Navy "E" award—for excellence), and my father's reputation, Shelburne Shipyard was quickly added to the Navy's bidders list.

The following summer, after graduating from Georgetown Preparatory School and passing the University of Vermont entrance exams, I was hired as a deckhand on the Ticonderoga, which had just been purchased by the Shelburne Museum. That was probably the best summer job a young guy could ever hope to have. Every day was wonderful, but one in particular was especially memorable. On the Ti's first run into the "Inland Sea" (the eastern side of the Champlain Islands) since before the War, on June 17, 1951, we passed the Horace Corbin estate on the western shore of South Hero. As was their custom, pilot Marty Fisher and his dad, Captain Alanson Fisher, blew the Ti's whistle, and Mr. Corbin, as usual, came out of the house and returned the salute with a vigorous wave. Following a successful celebratory cruise around the inland sea, on our return trip from St. Albans we struck the support structure of the railway bridge while exiting the so-called "Gut" (between the highway and railroad causeways), sustaining severe damage to the ship's forward port side. The liquor bar, which had so recently been filled with patrons, was jammed upwards along with the deck at a nearly thirty-degree angle. Mercifully, all the St. Albans passengers had disembarked before we started home or there would have been casualties. Pilot Fisher was forced to alter his intended course through the narrow opening by some stubborn fishermen who ignored repeated blasts from Ti's whistle. Knowing a collision was inevitable, Fisher made a hasty decision: He intentionally steered the forward section of the ship into the massive stone structure, thereby saving the paddle wheel from damage. From my vantage point on the forward promenade deck, I saw huge stones being peeled away and crashing into the water very close to one boatload of fishermen who had ignored the warnings. As their boat was swamped and they were thrown into the water, they must have become instant believers in the "Inland Waterway Rules of the Road." Some of us ran aft and threw life preservers to the hapless anglers, but that was all we could do. The Ti had such momentum that I don't recall even the slightest shudder as we made contact, and then we were through the gap

Fred Barrett checks George Darling's work on a captain's gig.

and on our way again as though nothing had happened. Thanks to Marty's courageous decision there had been no damage to the paddle wheel or the hull itself, and the shipyard crew Dad sent to make repairs had us back in operation within a week. Coincidentally, as we passed Horace Corbin's on the way back to Burlington there was no response to Marty's whistle. We learned later that, sadly, Corbin had suffered a fatal heart attack soon after our morning passage.

In 1952, our Shelburne Shipyard was awarded a contract for seventy-three 35-foot motorboats, commonly known as "admirals' barges" or "captain's gigs." My summer job in 1952 was assisting Ray Sargent while he lofted the gigs. This procedure consists of transferring the architect's drawings to full-scale lines using his table of offsets. It is usually done in the attic, or loft, where there is unobstructed open space. It was hot up there that summer so we worked in shorts and socks and used a lot of my mother's bath towels in a valiant, but usually unsuccessful, effort to keep our patterns dry. Our bible was Howard I. Chapelle's classic book Boatbuilding. We referred

*Jerry Aske, Jr.*

One of 73 captain's gigs ready for shipment to Navy base.

to it often, as this was Ray's first crack at lofting.

The yard turned out two captain's gigs per week using production techniques designed by my dad. The Navy brass were so impressed by the unit costs that they engaged one of our subcontractors to furnish the aluminum canopies—two per boat—for their own shipyards. Little did they know the embarrassing saga of those canopies. Ray Sargent had lofted their plans, too, and the finished molds had been sent to our subcontractor in Ohio (there being no local company capable of producing them). When the first units were delivered and lowered onto the deck of the prototype hull, they overhung the openings by exactly six inches on each side. As Ray tells the story, my dad knew that a major, and perhaps costly, mistake had been made, but he didn't fuss or fume or seem particularly upset. He just told Ray to take the next train to Ohio and solve the problem. After studying it for a few minutes he arrived at a very simple solution—cut a foot-wide chunk out of the middle of each mold! The subcontractor ownership was very impressed. Why couldn't their people have come up with such an obvious solution? Even though this contract was awarded after a competitive bidding process, and these were the least expensive gigs the US Navy had ever purchased (including those built in their own shipyards), upon its completion government bureaucrats concluded that we had made too much profit. Under procurement rules then in effect they could renegotiate our contract—even though it

Dad purchased countless marine items through Chiott's, rather than going directly to manufacturers. We collaborated later at boat shows.

was not a negotiated contract in the first place.

These captain's gigs did not need to be delivered by water. They were trucked to the Rutland Railroad siding in Shelburne where they were loaded on flatcars for delivery to the Navy. We erected our own crane there that we used for transferring from truck to track. This contract kept nearly fifty skilled shipyard workers busy until late 1954. As usual, my father did his best to purchase locally. Rather than go out of state for marine hardware, for instance, he opted to pay a little more and buy it from Chiott's Marine in Burlington.

The Korean War was over by the time the last gig was delivered, but a bid had already been accepted for 467 LCVPs (Landing Craft Vehicle and Personnel), or, as they were called during World War II, "Higgins boats." Again, as in that war, a Navy contract couldn't have come at a better time for the local economy. The Burlington Free Press headline on Saturday, December 18, 1954 read: "$3,500,000 contract means work for about 100, Building 472 craft." The shipyard usually employed fifteen men; the project would mean about fifty new hires. What my dad didn't tell the reporter was that a mathematical error he made during preparation of the bid would cost the company practically all its anticipated profit. I was in the office when our bookkeeper, Charlie Quinn, discovered the error. Our proposal had already been

LCVP being hoisted onto
Rutland Railroad flatcar
for shipment to Navy.

submitted and accepted. No wonder we were the low bidder! Dad was absolutely
devastated and we all shared his pain and embarrassment. But he went back to the
drawing boards determined to compensate for his error. In the end he devised even
more cost-saving production methods and saved the day.

Just the challenge of moving a boat every day—from the production line to
the lake for trials and sling testing and then to the truck for transport to the railroad
station—cried out for innovation (the "Subchaser Railroad" just wouldn't do). This
innovation came in the form of a revolutionary invention called a Travelift. (The owners of what would become the highly successful Travelift Company had constructed
one for their own use, but ours was the first one they sold to an outside firm.) A far
cry from today's self-propelled hydraulic models that can lift boats weighing more

Shipyard's first Travelift—the world's second—with a private yacht in slings.

than 100 tons, this was towed by a fifth-wheel cab (like a semi truck), could handle twelve tons, and the lift motors were electric. But it did the trick, shaving hours off that daily task. Although the original contract was for 472 boats, the number was later cut back to 467.

Production soon reached the rate of one per day. These boats were also shipped from Shelburne by rail. A dozen or so flatcars were permanently fitted with cradles and the Rutland Railroad always kept at least a week's supply on the siding so we could load them on a daily basis. A train would drop off a batch of empty cars about once a week, picking up a load of boats at the same time. Perhaps this arrangement was all that kept the Rutland Railroad in business, for it folded soon after we shipped the last LCVP.

The one-a-day production rate was the goal my dad had counted on when he submitted his bid to BUSHIPS, but from start to finish he had to put up with the new senior officer over at SUPSHIPS - Bath. Captain Alexander, apparently unwilling to take our past performance into account, recommended against us getting the contract because, in his judgment, Shelburne Shipyard was not a "responsible bidder." His feathers were ruffled when his superiors in Washington overruled him and awarded the contract to us. After that he did his level best to make our life as difficult as possible, no doubt hoping we would fail and the job would be turned over to the New

*Jerry Aske, Jr.*

Old railroad track storage yard in the pre-Travelift days.

England boatyard that he favored.

One of my first chores after graduating from the University of Vermont was to truck the plywood we had stockpiled for the entire project from our outside storage site to a vacant barn Dad rented from Derrick Webb over on Shelburne Farms. Never mind that this plywood was resin-impregnated, paper overlay, marine grade, and we had painted all the exposed edges just to be sure there would be no water damage. Even our civilian resident inspector, Ed Sonia, tried to convince Alexander that the product would be completely safe outdoors—but to no avail. Besides, at that point the plywood was ours! If it were damaged in any way we would have to replace it at our expense. This was harassment, borne out of pique, pure and simple.

Next, the good Captain tried to prevent BUSHIPS from approving a change order to substitute mahogany with marine plywood reinforcing gussets for the specified oak floor frames. We won that round (and so did the Navy, for that matter, because these floors were much stronger than the ones the specs called for).

The height of absurdity came when we were ordered to drill a pilot hole for every screw and, using an oilcan, squirt the wood preservative Cuprinol into each one before driving the screws. The use of impact drivers made pre-drilling unnecessary, and squirting a preservative into each and every hole was overkill of ridiculous proportions, especially when you consider that this model boat was supposed to be cheap and expendable. Taking into account the huge number of screw fasteners used in the construction of these boats, Alexander's requirement would have nearly doubled the production schedule Dad had worked so hard to achieve. Thankfully, Mr. Sonia turned a blind eye when the men bypassed this step.

Alexander's attitude even spilled over to one of his lieutenants. This young officer's hobby was collecting antique firearms. One day he approached my dad with a proposal that came very close to bribery. He not too subtly let it be known that he very much admired a certain matched pair of dueling pistols that were for sale at Wally White's gun shop on Shelburne Road. In the next breath he suggested that he had been considering overlooking some of the Captain's more onerous rules. Needless to say, the lieutenant did not return to Bath with a matched pair of dueling pistols!

Capt. Alexander got a taste of his own medicine, though, when he came over to observe the first boat's sea trials. Before sending the prototype to our subcontractor, Dad had asked if he might change the handle on the ramp latch assembly. It would be just a simple bend that would prevent possible injury when the latch came over the cam and snapped into place. Because the change would be made prior to manufacture, there would be no additional cost. True to form, Alexander objected and told my father to "build them according to the plans!" Guess who closed the starboard latch after the ramp test? As he freed the Captain's fingers, our guy Ray Cootware could hardly contain himself. Indeed, it was he who had suggested the change in the first place after getting caught in this "bear trap" himself while working on the prototype. Hardly a surprise, then, when we received a change order to redesign the handle like Dad had suggested—but now that all 467 pairs had been manufactured and delivered, the change cost the Navy a considerable sum.

Dad had to put up with some pettiness on the local level, too. On June 12, Inspector Sonia asked the Coast Guard station chief in Burlington to warn boat owners to stay clear of the LCVP test areas. Accordingly, a small notice ran in the Burlington Free Press to that effect. The very next day the Coast Guard scuttled the Navy warning, stating in the paper that owners of small boats had a right to anchor anywhere they liked. Rolla Hill, the man in charge of the local Coast Guard station, was quoted as saying, "No law says that a man can't sit out there in his boat and fish. If his anchored boat is swamped by a Navy boat, the Navy is just as liable as anyone else—and maybe a little bit more." Apparently he had received a number of phone calls from some annoyed anglers. So, two days later, the Free Press ran this letter from my dad:

It was never intended by the Navy or the Shipyard that the rights of fishermen or private boat operators in Shelburne Bay or anywhere else on Lake Champlain would be infringed upon or curtailed in any way, shape or manner.

The Shipyard, the Coast Guard Station, and the Naval Reserve Station have been deluged with phone calls protesting what one fisherman, who would not identify himself, called high-handed infringement on the rights of the public. It is most unfortunate, but the matter has become controversial without good reason.

Mr. Sonia, the Navy trial official at the Shelburne Shipyard, called Mr. Hill of the Coast Guard, requesting that fishermen and boatmen be advised of the daily trials that are being run and that they be asked to cooperate in the avoidance of accidents through the exercise of a little extra caution between noon and about 3 p.m. when the trials are usually run.

There was no intention to bar anyone from normal use of the waters of Shelburne Bay or anywhere else on the lake. As a matter of fact, there is no set course over which the trials are run. The trial course is determined from day to day depending upon wind and weather conditions.

To the best of my knowledge, there has been only one incident in connection with the testing of 220 boats through June 11. On that date the trial crew inadvertently passed within about twenty yards of a fishing boat in Shelburne Bay, which prompted Mr. Sonia to request that the Coast Guard ask boatmen to help avoid accidents by being extra watchful during the early afternoon …We are doing everything we can … and as an extra precaution we have added a bow-watch to the trial crew since June 11.

We will also fly a flag hereafter, which is the international signal that the boat … is operating under special conditions which recommend caution on the part of nearby craft.

Test specifications … require that the LCVPs be operated without interruption for one hour at 1,800 revolutions, and that they be put through maneuverability tests in connection with the one hour endurance run. Interruptions which might be caused by other craft crossing our course or approaching in a dangerous fashion can make it necessary for us to start the one hour run over again.

In conclusion Dad said,

I am sure that all sensible boatmen will agree with me, and I am certain that no accident will occur unless some crackpot sets it up through carelessness or horseplay.

After publication of this letter the matter never came up again.

# 9

The LCVP contract occupied the major portion of the Shipyard's efforts until 1958. I returned to the yard after an active duty interval with the US Army and picked up where I had left off two years before: I had left in the early stages of the LCVP job and came back just in time to take part in its completion. In July 1958, while I was stationed in Bamberg, Germany, tensions were growing in Lebanon, and we were alerted for imminent deployment to the region. In the event, our marines were welcomed ashore with bouquets instead of bombs, much to our collective relief. But another pleasant surprise was recognizing as Shelburne-built the landing craft in a widely circulated photograph of disembarking marines. The altered ramp latch assembly was a dead giveaway!

My folks met us in New York City the day we arrived from Germany, just before Christmas 1958. As early as that first evening, sitting in the Biltmore cocktail lounge, Dad and I had a rather heated discussion about the future of the shipyard. I felt that Navy work in peacetime was too uncertain and that we should turn exclusively to the private boating business. This had been my choice ever since the days when I would tie transient pleasure boats to the old timber barges that were half sunk at the south end of the harbor. I was adamant that if I were to stay with the company we would need to chart a new course. Dad confessed that, ever since the "renegotiation" dispute, and then the unpleasantness of Alexander's watch, he had seriously considered an end to government work. Despite earlier personal assurances during a meeting with Admiral Mumma—then Chief of BUSHIPS—that better procurement practices were being implemented, and the admiral's wish that Shelburne would remain on the government's bidders list, Dad agreed with me that it was time to move on.

Accordingly, the Shelburne Harbor Marina was born in the spring of 1959. Uncle Wendell was unhappy with this change in direction and soon sold us his shares of stock. Another unhappy person was Ken Lonergan, the owner of Champlain Marine in Mallets Bay. He obviously feared competition would hurt his business. In fact, the very opposite turned out to be the case. As word spread about the expanding facilities on Lake Champlain, more and more boaters headed north for their summer cruises. Entire US Power Squadrons began to include Lake Champlain in their summer cruising plans. The inaugural year of the new marina was a huge success. At the end of our first season we received the Inland Waterway Guide's "Best All-Around Marina" award for the Great Lakes area (of which Lake Champlain, strangely, is a part) "for outstanding service and unselfish promotion of boating."

View of the Shipyard when I returned from the Army near the end of our LCVP contract. Old barges and boardinghouse in the left foreground.

A popular feature of the marina was our Captain's Table restaurant. In those days nearly all our boating customers were transients from up and down the eastern seaboard, and they welcomed the chance to enjoy some drinks and meals ashore after days of galley fare. Every table was a front row seat overlooking the harbor, and we were fortunate to have found a wonderful chef who did not require a year-round job: Ken Harvey and his wife, Marge, were retired from the exclusive Owls Club in St. Albans. When we offered them lodging in the middle apartment of the "block" for the summer, they jumped at the chance to work for us. Not only did they help entice transients to return year after year, they also attracted a substantial following of their former St. Albans clients.

The Shipyard also benefited greatly from the marina. Many of those "downcountry" boaters managed to find their way onto Lake Champlain's many reefs, despite the fact that they are all identified on the US Coast and Geodetic Survey navigation charts and clearly marked with buoys on the water. We sent Ray Cootware to the Columbian Bronze Company's headquarters in Freeport, Long Island, to learn the art of propeller reconditioning. We also stocked blank propeller shafting to be cut, tapered, and keyed for replacements. It seems like there were always one or two boats hauled

*Jerry Aske, Jr.*

Burning the old barges to clear the way for new marina docks. Father and son confer, far right.

out either in the Travelift slings or on the Crandall railway. Our reputation with the insurance companies was impeccable, so much so that we never had to wait for an adjuster to come to Shelburne before we could proceed with repairs. Needless to say, this made for some very happy customers who dreaded every moment deducted from their vacations. Despite the distances and inconveniences involved, more than a few out-of-staters came to our yard for major mechanical and carpenter work just because of our widespread reputation for quality workmanship.

Not everyone was impressed by our naïve Vermont honesty, however. I encountered a few professional captains who asked for their "captain's commissions." At first I didn't know what that meant, but it became clear soon enough. Simply put, it means overbilling the insurance companies to pay off the captains for bringing their boats to us. Of course I refused, so initially a few captains grew angry and threatened to avoid our marina. But it didn't take long for the word to get around that we weren't to be bought, and not only the boat owners came to respect our Vermont honesty, but the captains did as well. I hasten to add that it wasn't just hired captains who thought it was perfectly okay to cheat an insurance company; some owners did, too.

One day in 1961 or 1962 a man came to my office seeking advice on moving a

Spraying diesel fuel on barges to hasten burning.

Revolutionary War gunboat. The man turned out to be none other that the author of our lofting bible, Howard Chapelle! I could barely hide my excitement and awe. The gunboat, *Philadelphia*, was to be moved from Westport, New York to the Smithsonian Institution in Washington, D.C. From the time of its sinking during the Battle of Valcour in 1776 until its recovery off the southwestern end of Valcour Island in 1935, this historic artifact had been well-preserved by the cold, fresh waters of Lake Champlain. After being floated to the surface, she was towed to the shipyard and hauled out of the water on the Crandall railway. There, a barge was built around her so she could be taken around the lake for public display. During the intervening years, exposure to the elements—oxygen, especially—had taken its toll. *Philadelphia* was bequeathed to the Smithsonian just in time to save her from complete decay. I suggested Mr. Chapelle engage the Champlain Transportation Company lighter, load it on a barge, and float it all the way to Washington. He agreed that was a sensible idea and that's what they did. Now the chemically preserved original *Philadelphia* is on exhibition at the Smithsonian's National Museum of American History. A full-scale replica of *Philadelphia* is currently afloat at the Lake Champlain Maritime Museum at Basin Harbor, Vermont.

The success of the marina was not to spell the end of boat construction at the

*Jerry Aske, Jr.*

Dad, with Miss Vermont, accepting the *Inland Waterway Guide's* "Best All Around Marina for 1959, Great Lakes Area" award.

yard, however. Early in 1965 we entered into a contract with the Pembroke Boat Company of Suncook, New Hampshire, to build one of their line of sea skiff cruisers. Due to the increasing popularity of their boats, Pembroke simply could not satisfy demand. Since we had been Pembroke dealers for some time, the owners had come to know us personally and were aware of our past production record and reputation for quality. They decided the only way to increase production was to farm out the 23-foot cruiser to us.

A separate labor force was recruited under the guidance of Jack Lance, our general yard and production superintendent. Lance spent two months at the Suncook plant working on their production line and learning their system. He returned to the shipyard with all the jigs and patterns for the 23-foot model. Over the next year-and-a-half we built fifty Pembroke 23s. At the conclusion of that contract we took on the production of another popular 23-foot sea skiff line, this time for the Henry Luhrs boatyard of Morgan, New Jersey. Although we didn't build it, we did arrange the purchase of a custom-built 27-foot Luhrs for the newly created State Police Marine Division. Sergeant Harold "Red" Dean and I personally visited the Luhrs plant and drew up the specifications for that craft with old Henry Luhrs.

Marina bar and lounge on second deck. Tugboat *General Allen*'s steering wheel in the ceiling.

The marina's first season, 1958. *Ticonderoga's* winter dock in the foreground, which would become an anchor for my marina. The dock on pilings was originally built for Horace Corbin's yacht, *Chevela*.

*Jerry Aske, Jr.*

Bird's-eye view of the new marina.

While we no longer did Navy work, a perennial source of amusement for us was a recurring springtime job for another branch of our government. That involved replacing the perpetually rotting planks on the US Coast Guard's buoy boat. This was always good for several days' work at government expense. To this day I cannot understand their reluctance to simply replace the whole boat. This old gal is now a permanent resident at the Lake Champlain Maritime Museum, a reminder of the good old times when wooden ships ruled the waves of Lake Champlain.

# Epilogue

In 1968 we sold the Shelburne Shipyard to Burlington bankers Horace Ransom and Robert Montgomery. A couple of years later it was purchased by the Griswold family, the current owners. We retained the residential properties and the corporate charter, and today—with the Griswolds' cooperation—my wife Margaret and I operate a smaller marina directly adjacent to the Shipyard's.

Our home overlooks the dock where I first saw *Vermont III*, later the winter berth for *Ticonderoga,* until her move to the Shelburne Museum. Records show the building was converted to a dwelling in 1890, but according to Fred Barrett, who spent most of his life at the shipyard and whose father was foreman in the late nineteenth century, it was originally a shipyard carpenter shop. Although Fred didn't know the original date of construction, when we remodeled in 1972 we discovered an undated section of newspaper pasted against the outer sheathing of one wall with an editorial debating the prospects of Lincoln's re-election! So we can be reasonably certain that this portion of our house was built sometime before 1864. Fred raised his family in this house, and it became the shipyard's third dwelling to have indoor plumbing when he recycled one of the bathrooms from *Vermont III*. The dock is the access and anchor to our floating marina system and, again according to Fred, sits atop an old skid railway. The position of certain timbers protruding from beneath the dock would seem to confirm his contention.

Today, the streets of the Harborwood Shores residential subdivision that my father created out of some of our unused acreage in 1971 are reminders of the old days with the names *General Greene, Chateaugay,* and *Ticonderoga.*

Today, the Shipyard builds no wooden boats or ships.

Today, the US Navy *owns* no wooden boats or ships—except for the *USS Constitution,* from the days of fighting sail!

www.ingramcontent.com/pod-product-compliance
Lightning Source LLC
Chambersburg PA
CBHW041540120626
46551CB00019B/2779